50 Fresh and Tasty Smoothies

By: Kelly Johnson

Table of Contents

- Tropical Mango Smoothie
- Green Detox Smoothie
- Berry Blast Smoothie
- Pineapple Coconut Smoothie
- Strawberry Banana Smoothie
- Avocado and Spinach Smoothie
- Blueberry Almond Smoothie
- Raspberry Peach Smoothie
- Kiwi Lime Smoothie
- Watermelon Mint Smoothie
- Tropical Green Smoothie
- Acai Berry Smoothie
- Chocolate Banana Smoothie
- Papaya Mango Smoothie
- Orange Carrot Ginger Smoothie
- Pomegranate Berry Smoothie
- Coconut Berry Smoothie
- Protein-Packed Peanut Butter Smoothie
- Cucumber Melon Smoothie
- Cherry Almond Smoothie
- Mango Coconut Smoothie
- Apple Cinnamon Smoothie
- Green Apple Kiwi Smoothie
- Pineapple Ginger Smoothie
- Strawberry Kiwi Smoothie
- Pear and Spinach Smoothie
- Almond Butter Banana Smoothie
- Papaya Pineapple Smoothie
- Cantaloupe Mint Smoothie
- Blueberry Spinach Smoothie
- Avocado Mango Smoothie
- Peachy Green Smoothie
- Coconut Matcha Smoothie
- Superfood Smoothie
- Mango Chia Smoothie

- Banana Oat Smoothie
- Beetroot Berry Smoothie
- Carrot Orange Smoothie
- Chocolate Cherry Smoothie
- Pineapple Passionfruit Smoothie
- Coconut Lime Smoothie
- Apricot Almond Smoothie
- Cinnamon Apple Smoothie
- Lemon Berry Smoothie
- Coconut Mango Smoothie
- Papaya Mint Smoothie
- Apple Pear Smoothie
- Honeydew Kiwi Smoothie
- Coconut Raspberry Smoothie
- Matcha Coconut Smoothie

Tropical Mango Smoothie

Ingredients:

- 1 ripe mango, peeled and diced
- 1/2 cup pineapple chunks
- 1/2 cup coconut milk
- 1/4 cup orange juice
- 1/2 cup ice cubes

Instructions:

1. Blend all ingredients in a blender until smooth.
2. Pour into a glass and enjoy!

Green Detox Smoothie

Ingredients:

- 1/2 cucumber, chopped
- 1 cup spinach
- 1 green apple, cored and chopped
- 1/2 lemon, juiced
- 1 tablespoon ginger, grated
- 1 cup coconut water
- 1/2 cup ice cubes

Instructions:

1. Add all ingredients to a blender and blend until smooth.
2. Pour into a glass and serve chilled.

Berry Blast Smoothie

Ingredients:

- 1/2 cup strawberries
- 1/2 cup blueberries
- 1/2 cup raspberries
- 1/2 cup Greek yogurt
- 1 tablespoon honey (optional)
- 1/2 cup almond milk
- 1/2 cup ice cubes

Instructions:

1. Place all ingredients into a blender and blend until smooth.
2. Pour into a glass and enjoy immediately.

Pineapple Coconut Smoothie

Ingredients:

- 1 cup pineapple chunks
- 1/2 cup coconut milk
- 1/4 cup Greek yogurt
- 1 tablespoon shredded coconut
- 1/2 cup ice cubes

Instructions:

1. Blend all ingredients together in a blender until smooth.
2. Serve in a glass and garnish with additional coconut if desired.

Strawberry Banana Smoothie

Ingredients:

- 1 ripe banana
- 1/2 cup strawberries
- 1/2 cup Greek yogurt
- 1/4 cup almond milk
- 1 teaspoon honey (optional)
- 1/2 cup ice cubes

Instructions:

1. Add all ingredients to a blender and blend until smooth.
2. Pour into a glass and enjoy!

Avocado and Spinach Smoothie

Ingredients:

- 1/2 avocado, peeled and pitted
- 1 cup spinach
- 1/2 banana
- 1/2 cup almond milk
- 1 tablespoon chia seeds
- 1/2 cup ice cubes

Instructions:

1. Place all ingredients in a blender and blend until smooth.
2. Pour into a glass and serve immediately.

Blueberry Almond Smoothie

Ingredients:

- 1/2 cup blueberries
- 1 tablespoon almond butter
- 1/2 cup almond milk
- 1/2 cup Greek yogurt
- 1 teaspoon honey (optional)
- 1/2 cup ice cubes

Instructions:

1. Blend all ingredients in a blender until smooth.
2. Pour into a glass and enjoy!

Raspberry Peach Smoothie

Ingredients:

- 1/2 cup raspberries
- 1 ripe peach, sliced
- 1/2 cup Greek yogurt
- 1/4 cup orange juice
- 1 tablespoon honey (optional)
- 1/2 cup ice cubes

Instructions:

1. Place all ingredients in a blender and blend until smooth.
2. Pour into a glass and enjoy!

Kiwi Lime Smoothie

Ingredients:

- 2 ripe kiwis, peeled and chopped
- 1/2 cup pineapple chunks
- 1 tablespoon lime juice
- 1/2 cup coconut water
- 1/2 cup ice cubes

Instructions:

1. Combine all ingredients in a blender and blend until smooth.
2. Pour into a glass and enjoy!

Watermelon Mint Smoothie

Ingredients:

- 2 cups watermelon, cubed
- 1/2 cup Greek yogurt
- 1 tablespoon fresh mint leaves
- 1/2 cup coconut water
- 1/2 cup ice cubes

Instructions:

1. Blend watermelon, yogurt, mint leaves, coconut water, and ice cubes until smooth.
2. Pour into a glass, garnish with a mint sprig, and enjoy!

Tropical Green Smoothie

Ingredients:

- 1/2 cup pineapple chunks
- 1/2 cup mango chunks
- 1 cup spinach
- 1/2 banana
- 1 cup coconut water
- 1/2 cup ice cubes

Instructions:

1. Add pineapple, mango, spinach, banana, coconut water, and ice cubes to a blender.
2. Blend until smooth and serve immediately.

Acai Berry Smoothie

Ingredients:

- 1 packet acai berry puree (or 1/2 cup acai powder)
- 1/2 cup blueberries
- 1/2 banana
- 1/2 cup almond milk
- 1 tablespoon honey (optional)
- 1/2 cup ice cubes

Instructions:

1. Blend acai puree or powder with blueberries, banana, almond milk, honey, and ice cubes.
2. Pour into a glass and enjoy!

Chocolate Banana Smoothie

Ingredients:

- 1 ripe banana
- 1 tablespoon unsweetened cocoa powder
- 1/2 cup almond milk
- 1/2 cup Greek yogurt
- 1 teaspoon honey or maple syrup
- 1/2 cup ice cubes

Instructions:

1. Add banana, cocoa powder, almond milk, Greek yogurt, honey, and ice cubes to a blender.
2. Blend until smooth and serve immediately.

Papaya Mango Smoothie

Ingredients:

- 1 cup papaya, peeled and chopped
- 1/2 cup mango chunks
- 1/2 cup coconut milk
- 1 tablespoon lime juice
- 1/2 cup ice cubes

Instructions:

1. Combine papaya, mango, coconut milk, lime juice, and ice cubes in a blender.
2. Blend until smooth and enjoy!

Orange Carrot Ginger Smoothie

Ingredients:

- 2 oranges, peeled and segmented
- 1/2 cup carrot juice or 1/2 cup fresh carrots
- 1 teaspoon fresh ginger, grated
- 1/2 cup coconut water
- 1/2 cup ice cubes

Instructions:

1. Blend all ingredients together until smooth.
2. Pour into a glass and enjoy the refreshing smoothie!

Pomegranate Berry Smoothie

Ingredients:

- 1/2 cup pomegranate seeds
- 1/2 cup blueberries
- 1/2 cup raspberries
- 1/2 banana
- 1/2 cup Greek yogurt
- 1/2 cup almond milk
- 1/2 cup ice cubes

Instructions:

1. Add pomegranate seeds, berries, banana, Greek yogurt, almond milk, and ice cubes to a blender.
2. Blend until smooth and serve!

Coconut Berry Smoothie

Ingredients:

- 1/2 cup strawberries
- 1/2 cup blueberries
- 1/4 cup shredded coconut
- 1/2 cup coconut milk
- 1/2 cup Greek yogurt
- 1/2 cup ice cubes

Instructions:

1. Blend berries, shredded coconut, coconut milk, Greek yogurt, and ice cubes until smooth.
2. Serve chilled, garnished with extra coconut if desired.

Protein-Packed Peanut Butter Smoothie

Ingredients:

- 2 tablespoons peanut butter
- 1 ripe banana
- 1/2 cup Greek yogurt
- 1 tablespoon chia seeds
- 1/2 cup almond milk
- 1/2 cup ice cubes

Instructions:

1. Blend peanut butter, banana, Greek yogurt, chia seeds, almond milk, and ice cubes.
2. Blend until smooth and serve immediately for a protein-packed treat!

Cucumber Melon Smoothie

Ingredients:

- 1/2 cucumber, peeled and chopped
- 1 cup honeydew melon or cantaloupe, chopped
- 1/2 cup Greek yogurt
- 1 tablespoon lime juice
- 1/2 cup coconut water
- 1/2 cup ice cubes

Instructions:

1. Blend cucumber, melon, Greek yogurt, lime juice, coconut water, and ice cubes until smooth.
2. Pour into a glass and serve chilled.

Cherry Almond Smoothie

Ingredients:

- 1 cup cherries, pitted (fresh or frozen)
- 1 tablespoon almond butter
- 1/2 cup almond milk
- 1/2 teaspoon vanilla extract
- 1/2 cup Greek yogurt
- 1/2 cup ice cubes

Instructions:

1. Blend cherries, almond butter, almond milk, vanilla extract, Greek yogurt, and ice cubes.
2. Blend until smooth and serve immediately.

Mango Coconut Smoothie

Ingredients:

- 1 cup mango chunks
- 1/2 cup coconut milk
- 1/4 cup shredded coconut
- 1 tablespoon honey or maple syrup (optional)
- 1/2 cup ice cubes

Instructions:

1. Combine mango, coconut milk, shredded coconut, honey, and ice cubes in a blender.
2. Blend until smooth, pour into a glass, and garnish with extra coconut if desired.

Apple Cinnamon Smoothie

Ingredients:

- 1 apple, cored and chopped
- 1/2 teaspoon ground cinnamon
- 1/2 cup Greek yogurt
- 1/2 cup almond milk
- 1 tablespoon honey (optional)
- 1/2 cup ice cubes

Instructions:

1. Add apple, cinnamon, Greek yogurt, almond milk, honey, and ice cubes to a blender.
2. Blend until smooth and enjoy!

Green Apple Kiwi Smoothie

Ingredients:

- 1 green apple, cored and chopped
- 2 kiwis, peeled and chopped
- 1/2 cup spinach
- 1/2 cup coconut water
- 1 tablespoon honey (optional)
- 1/2 cup ice cubes

Instructions:

1. Blend apple, kiwi, spinach, coconut water, honey, and ice cubes until smooth.
2. Pour into a glass and serve immediately.

Pineapple Ginger Smoothie

Ingredients:

- 1 cup pineapple chunks
- 1/2 teaspoon fresh ginger, grated
- 1/2 cup coconut milk
- 1/2 cup Greek yogurt
- 1/2 cup ice cubes

Instructions:

1. Combine pineapple, ginger, coconut milk, Greek yogurt, and ice cubes in a blender.
2. Blend until smooth and serve chilled.

Strawberry Kiwi Smoothie

Ingredients:

- 1/2 cup strawberries
- 2 kiwis, peeled and chopped
- 1/2 cup Greek yogurt
- 1/2 cup almond milk
- 1/2 cup ice cubes

Instructions:

1. Add strawberries, kiwi, Greek yogurt, almond milk, and ice cubes to a blender.
2. Blend until smooth, pour into a glass, and enjoy!

Pear and Spinach Smoothie

Ingredients:

- 1 ripe pear, cored and chopped
- 1/2 cup spinach
- 1/2 banana
- 1/2 cup almond milk
- 1 tablespoon honey (optional)
- 1/2 cup ice cubes

Instructions:

1. Blend pear, spinach, banana, almond milk, honey, and ice cubes until smooth.
2. Pour into a glass and enjoy!

Almond Butter Banana Smoothie

Ingredients:

- 1 ripe banana
- 1 tablespoon almond butter
- 1/2 cup almond milk
- 1/2 teaspoon vanilla extract
- 1/2 cup Greek yogurt
- 1/2 cup ice cubes

Instructions:

1. Blend banana, almond butter, almond milk, vanilla extract, Greek yogurt, and ice cubes.
2. Blend until smooth and serve immediately.

Papaya Pineapple Smoothie

Ingredients:

- 1 cup papaya, peeled and chopped
- 1/2 cup pineapple chunks
- 1/2 cup coconut water
- 1 tablespoon honey (optional)
- 1/2 cup ice cubes

Instructions:

1. Blend papaya, pineapple, coconut water, honey, and ice cubes until smooth.
2. Serve chilled and enjoy!

Cantaloupe Mint Smoothie

Ingredients:

- 1 cup cantaloupe, peeled and chopped
- 1/4 cup fresh mint leaves
- 1/2 cup Greek yogurt
- 1 tablespoon honey (optional)
- 1/2 cup ice cubes

Instructions:

1. Blend cantaloupe, mint, Greek yogurt, honey, and ice cubes until smooth.
2. Pour into a glass, garnish with mint leaves, and enjoy!

Blueberry Spinach Smoothie

Ingredients:

- 1/2 cup blueberries (fresh or frozen)
- 1/2 cup spinach
- 1/2 banana
- 1/2 cup almond milk
- 1 tablespoon chia seeds
- 1/2 cup ice cubes

Instructions:

1. Add blueberries, spinach, banana, almond milk, chia seeds, and ice cubes to a blender.
2. Blend until smooth and serve immediately.

Avocado Mango Smoothie

Ingredients:

- 1/2 ripe avocado, peeled and pitted
- 1/2 cup mango chunks
- 1/2 cup coconut milk
- 1 tablespoon honey or maple syrup (optional)
- 1/2 cup ice cubes

Instructions:

1. Blend avocado, mango, coconut milk, honey, and ice cubes until smooth.
2. Pour into a glass and enjoy!

Peachy Green Smoothie

Ingredients:

- 1 ripe peach, pitted and chopped
- 1/2 cup spinach
- 1/2 banana
- 1/2 cup coconut water
- 1 tablespoon honey (optional)
- 1/2 cup ice cubes

Instructions:

1. Add peach, spinach, banana, coconut water, honey, and ice cubes to a blender.
2. Blend until smooth and enjoy this refreshing smoothie!

Coconut Matcha Smoothie

Ingredients:

- 1/2 teaspoon matcha powder
- 1/2 cup coconut milk
- 1/2 banana
- 1 tablespoon honey or maple syrup (optional)
- 1/2 cup ice cubes

Instructions:

1. Blend matcha powder, coconut milk, banana, honey, and ice cubes until smooth.
2. Pour into a glass and enjoy!

Superfood Smoothie

Ingredients:

- 1/2 cup blueberries
- 1 tablespoon chia seeds
- 1 tablespoon flaxseeds
- 1/2 banana
- 1/2 cup almond milk
- 1/2 cup spinach
- 1/2 cup ice cubes

Instructions:

1. Blend blueberries, chia seeds, flaxseeds, banana, almond milk, spinach, and ice cubes until smooth.
2. Pour into a glass and enjoy the nutrient-packed smoothie!

Mango Chia Smoothie

Ingredients:

- 1 cup mango chunks
- 1 tablespoon chia seeds
- 1/2 cup coconut water
- 1/2 cup Greek yogurt
- 1/2 cup ice cubes

Instructions:

1. Blend mango, chia seeds, coconut water, Greek yogurt, and ice cubes until smooth.
2. Serve chilled and enjoy!

Banana Oat Smoothie

Ingredients:

- 1 ripe banana
- 1/4 cup rolled oats
- 1/2 cup almond milk
- 1 tablespoon almond butter
- 1/2 teaspoon cinnamon
- 1/2 cup ice cubes

Instructions:

1. Add banana, oats, almond milk, almond butter, cinnamon, and ice cubes to a blender.
2. Blend until smooth and serve immediately.

Beetroot Berry Smoothie

Ingredients:

- 1/2 cup cooked beetroot, peeled and chopped
- 1/2 cup mixed berries (strawberries, blueberries, raspberries)
- 1/2 banana
- 1/2 cup almond milk
- 1 tablespoon honey (optional)
- 1/2 cup ice cubes

Instructions:

1. Blend beetroot, mixed berries, banana, almond milk, honey, and ice cubes until smooth.
2. Pour into a glass and enjoy this vibrant, nutritious smoothie!

Carrot Orange Smoothie

Ingredients:

- 1 medium carrot, peeled and chopped
- 1 orange, peeled and segmented
- 1/2 banana
- 1/2 cup Greek yogurt
- 1/2 cup almond milk
- 1/2 cup ice cubes

Instructions:

1. Combine carrot, orange, banana, Greek yogurt, almond milk, and ice cubes in a blender.
2. Blend until smooth and enjoy!

Chocolate Cherry Smoothie

Ingredients:

- 1/2 cup cherries (fresh or frozen)
- 1 tablespoon cocoa powder
- 1/2 cup almond milk
- 1/2 banana
- 1 tablespoon honey or maple syrup (optional)
- 1/2 cup ice cubes

Instructions:

1. Add cherries, cocoa powder, almond milk, banana, honey, and ice cubes to a blender.
2. Blend until smooth and indulge in this chocolatey treat!

Pineapple Passionfruit Smoothie

Ingredients:

- 1/2 cup pineapple chunks
- 1 passionfruit, pulp scraped out
- 1/2 banana
- 1/2 cup coconut milk
- 1 tablespoon honey (optional)
- 1/2 cup ice cubes

Instructions:

1. Blend pineapple, passionfruit pulp, banana, coconut milk, honey, and ice cubes until smooth.
2. Serve chilled and enjoy the tropical flavors!

Coconut Lime Smoothie

Ingredients:

- 1/2 cup coconut milk
- 1 tablespoon shredded coconut
- 1/2 banana
- Juice of 1 lime
- 1/2 tablespoon honey (optional)
- 1/2 cup ice cubes

Instructions:

1. Blend coconut milk, shredded coconut, banana, lime juice, honey, and ice cubes until smooth.
2. Pour into a glass and enjoy this refreshing smoothie!

Apricot Almond Smoothie

Ingredients:

- 4 apricots, pitted and chopped
- 1 tablespoon almond butter
- 1/2 cup almond milk
- 1/2 banana
- 1/2 teaspoon vanilla extract
- 1/2 cup ice cubes

Instructions:

1. Combine apricots, almond butter, almond milk, banana, vanilla extract, and ice cubes in a blender.
2. Blend until smooth and serve immediately!

Cinnamon Apple Smoothie

Ingredients:

- 1 apple, cored and chopped
- 1/2 teaspoon ground cinnamon
- 1/2 cup Greek yogurt
- 1/2 cup almond milk
- 1 tablespoon honey (optional)
- 1/2 cup ice cubes

Instructions:

1. Blend apple, cinnamon, Greek yogurt, almond milk, honey, and ice cubes until smooth.
2. Pour into a glass, sprinkle with extra cinnamon, and enjoy!

Lemon Berry Smoothie

Ingredients:

- 1/2 cup mixed berries (strawberries, blueberries, raspberries)
- Juice of 1 lemon
- 1/2 banana
- 1/2 cup almond milk
- 1 tablespoon honey or maple syrup (optional)
- 1/2 cup ice cubes

Instructions:

1. Blend mixed berries, lemon juice, banana, almond milk, honey, and ice cubes until smooth.
2. Pour into a glass and serve chilled.

Coconut Mango Smoothie

Ingredients:

- 1/2 cup mango chunks
- 1/2 cup coconut milk
- 1 tablespoon shredded coconut
- 1/2 banana
- 1 tablespoon honey (optional)
- 1/2 cup ice cubes

Instructions:

1. Combine mango, coconut milk, shredded coconut, banana, honey, and ice cubes in a blender.
2. Blend until smooth and enjoy the tropical flavors!

Papaya Mint Smoothie

Ingredients:

- 1 cup papaya, peeled and chopped
- 1/4 cup fresh mint leaves
- 1/2 banana
- 1/2 cup coconut water
- 1 tablespoon honey (optional)
- 1/2 cup ice cubes

Instructions:

1. Blend papaya, mint, banana, coconut water, honey, and ice cubes until smooth.
2. Serve chilled and enjoy the refreshing flavors!

Apple Pear Smoothie

Ingredients:

- 1 apple, cored and chopped
- 1 pear, cored and chopped
- 1/2 banana
- 1/2 cup almond milk
- 1 tablespoon honey or maple syrup (optional)
- 1/2 cup ice cubes

Instructions:

1. Add apple, pear, banana, almond milk, honey, and ice cubes to a blender.
2. Blend until smooth and serve immediately.

Honeydew Kiwi Smoothie

Ingredients:

- 1 cup honeydew melon, peeled and chopped
- 1 kiwi, peeled and chopped
- 1/2 banana
- 1/2 cup coconut water
- 1 tablespoon honey (optional)
- 1/2 cup ice cubes

Instructions:

1. Combine honeydew melon, kiwi, banana, coconut water, honey, and ice cubes in a blender.
2. Blend until smooth and enjoy the sweet, tropical flavors!

Coconut Raspberry Smoothie

Ingredients:

- 1/2 cup coconut milk
- 1/2 cup raspberries (fresh or frozen)
- 1/2 banana
- 1 tablespoon honey (optional)
- 1/2 cup ice cubes

Instructions:

1. Blend coconut milk, raspberries, banana, honey, and ice cubes until smooth.
2. Pour into a glass and enjoy the creamy and fruity smoothie!

Matcha Coconut Smoothie

Ingredients:

- 1/2 teaspoon matcha powder
- 1/2 cup coconut milk
- 1/2 banana
- 1 tablespoon honey or maple syrup (optional)
- 1/2 cup ice cubes

Instructions:

1. Add matcha powder, coconut milk, banana, honey, and ice cubes to a blender.
2. Blend until smooth and serve chilled for a refreshing green smoothie!